Editor
Eric Migliaccio

Managing Editor
Ina Massler Levin, M.A.

Editor-in-Chief
Sharon Coan, M.S. Ed.

Illustrator
Sue Fullam

Cover Artist
Barb Lorseyedi

Art Coordinator
Kevin Barnes

Imaging
Rosa C. See

Product Manager
Phil Garcia

Publisher
Mary D. Smith, M.S. Ed.

Practice Makes Perfect

Writing Paragraphs

GRADE 6

I belong to:
Janine
Kwasniewski

Author

Wanda Kelly

Teacher Created Resources, Inc.
6421 Industry Way
Westminster, CA 92683
www.teachercreated.com
ISBN: 978-0-7439-3349-0

©2003 Teacher Created Resources, Inc.
Reprinted, 2008
Made in U.S.A.

Table of Contents

Introduction

This book has been written to help parents and teachers reinforce basic skills with children. *Practice Makes Perfect: Writing Paragraphs* reviews basic composition skills for sixth graders. The exercises in this book can be used sequentially or can be used out of order, as needed.

The following standards or objectives will be met or reinforced by completing the practice pages included in this book. These standards and objectives are similar to the ones required by your state and school district because they are considered appropriate for sixth graders.

- The student is familiar with the basic rules of grammar, punctuation, capitalization, and spelling.

- The student chooses effective vocabulary and uses figurative language in compositions.

- The student is able to vary sentence structures to improve the quality of a composition.

- The student can plan and compose a paragraph and use transitions to connect the paragraphs in an essay.

- The student can proofread paragraphs and essays by checking grammar, punctuation, capitalization, and spelling.

- The student can edit compositions to improve clarity, word choice, and language use.

- The student can choose topics for, organize, compose, proofread, edit, and evaluate the following kinds of essays consisting of a minimum of three paragraphs: expository, narrative, autobiographical, biographical, persuasive, book report.

- The student can compose business letters that request and respond.

- The student can evaluate paragraphs and essays, including those written by others.

Review the Basics

➤ Correct the grammar, punctuation, capitalization, and spelling errors in the following sentences. If there are no errors in a sentence, leave the line blank.

1. your the First One in your famly, to have a bicyle of your verry own.

   _____

2. Jane Smith Kim Choi and Sitara Jaworski went too lakewood mall two by knew cloths!

   _____

3. Pedro won! _____

4. They was the verry last wons too leeve the room on valentine's day.

   _____

5. Are you the air to your wealthy Uncles estate.

   _____

6. we dont want too go to the party latter.

   _____

7. Jerry had his papier with him; but he didnt have his pencil?

   _____

8. Ari isn't never going shoping with them girls agin.

   _____

9. There is hardly any diffrences between them three girls.

   _____

10. On independence day wee had went to the Colorado river with are friends.

    _____

11. hurry, hurry! mother yelled. I need help with them groceries.

    _____

12. Mother asked us to hurry and to help her with the groceries.

    _____

Assessment: The Basics

➤ In each group of sentences, choose the one that is correct by filling in the circle beside it.

1. (a) Wear are you going this afternoon?" asked his mother.
   (b) "Where are you going this afternoon," asked his mother.
   (c) "Where are you going this afternoon?" asked his mother.
   (d) "Where are you going this afternoon?" asked his Mother.

2. (a) There is ate students absent today?
   (b) Their are eight Students absent today.
   (c) There are eight students absent today.
   (d) There are eight students, absence today?

3. (a) Four Memorial Day we invited the neighborhood to a party.
   (b) For memorial day we invited the neighbor hood to a party.
   (c) Fore Memorial Day we invited the neighborhood to a party.
   (d) For Memorial Day we invited the neighborhood to a party.

4. (a) I like to go camping the last time we went I saw a bear.
   (b) I like to go camping; the last time we went, I saw a bear.
   (c) I like to go camping, the last time we went, I saw a bear.
   (d) I like to go camping the last time, we went, I saw a bear.

5. (a) Who's going to Spring Fling with Li!
   (b) Whose going to spring fling with Li?
   (c) Whose going to Spring Fling with Li!
   (d) Who's going to Spring Fling with Li?

6. (a) Akim! Dont due that!
   (b) Akim, Don't do that!
   (c) Akim! Don't do that!
   (d) Akim! Don't due that?

7. (a) It was on August 16, 1993, that she was born.
   (b) It wuz on August 16 1993 that she was borne.
   (c) It wass on august 16 1993 that she was born.
   (d) It was, on August 16, 1993, that she was born.

8. (a) Maria's favorite artists is Andrew Wyeth.
   (b) Marias favrite artist is Andrew Wyeth.
   (c) Marias favorite artists is Andrew Wyeth.
   (d) Maria's favorite artist is Andrew Wyeth.

Word Choice

➤ Replace the italicized words with more appropriate or more specific words. The first one has been done for you.

1. Sanford *said* that he would be *there* later.

   Sanford growled that he would be at Commonwealth Park later.
   _____

2. Josefina *liked* the *dress*.

   _____

3. Betty *walked* to the *store*.

   _____

4. The *music* was *terrific*.

   _____

5. Lim asked the *man* for *food*.

   _____

6. Beverly *ate* three *sandwiches*.

   _____

7. *Several children* skipped happily *away*.

   _____

8. Suzi thanked *her nicely*.

   _____

9. The *horse ran* around the corral.

   _____

10. Nowlan *talked* with the *pretty* fashion model.

    _____

11. Because he did not want to be late for *the important occasion*, he *ran*.

    _____

Sensory Words

Sensory words are words that describe how something *feels*, how something *looks*, how something *sounds*, how something *smells*, or how something *tastes*.

>   *example: The tang of the rhubarb made my tongue tingle.* taste (*tang*) and feel (*tingle*)

➤   Write a sentence that uses one of the five senses to describe each of the following. On the line after the sentence, write which of the senses you used.

1. pizza _____   _____

2. soccer ball _____   _____

3. camel _____   _____

4. sports announcer _____   _____

5. notebook _____   _____

6. tennis shoes _____   _____

7. desert _____   _____

8. beach _____   _____

9. surprise _____   _____

10. happiness _____   _____

11. embarrassment _____   _____

12. snake _____   _____

13. rock _____   _____

Figurative Language

✛ A *simile* is a direct comparison between two unrelated things, indicating a likeness that exists in one special way. A simile uses the words *like* or *as* to make the comparison.

✛ A *metaphor* is an indirect comparison between two unrelated things, indicating a likeness that exists in one special way. A metaphor does not use *like* or *as* to make a comparison. Instead, a metaphor states one thing acts like or appears to be another.

examples: *Our resident hummingbird looks like a helicopter at the feeder.* (**simile**)

Our resident hummingbird is a helicopter at the feeder. (**metaphor**)

➤ Create both a simile and a metaphor to describe each of the following:

1. a cat stalking a bird

_____

_____

2. a cowboy roping a calf

_____

_____

3. an alligator eating a fish

_____

_____

4. a student writing a paragraph

_____

_____

5. a girl skipping rope

_____

_____

6. a parent feeding a baby in a highchair

_____

_____

Sentence Variety

➤ In order to achieve sentence variety, change the order of the words in the following sentences without changing the meanings.

example: I strolled to the neighborhood supermarket this morning to buy some milk.
   This morning I strolled to the neighborhood supermarket to buy some milk.

1. Please do not go into the classroom without permission from the teacher.

   _____

   _____

2. Henri could not go to the baseball game because he had the measles.

   _____

   _____

3. After the campers finished eating the hotdogs and marshmallows they roasted over the fire, they sat around telling ghost stories.

   _____

   _____

4. Louise picked up about 12 pounds of rocks when she went walking on Mora Beach.

   _____

   _____

5. Some of the banana slugs in the Hoh Rain Forest on the Olympic Peninsula are a foot long. _____

   _____

6. Before Tina could go to the movies, she had to wash the dishes, finish her homework, and clean her room.

   _____

   _____

7. Nearly every day Fiona walks to school with her brother Ewan.

   _____

   _____

8. Every day from two until four in the afternoon, I practice playing the piano.

   _____

   _____

Assessment: Descriptive Language and Sentence Variety

Word Choice and Sentence Variety

➤ In each group of sentences, fill in the circle by the one that contains the most detailed description.

1. (a) Cheerful Allison happily skipped to busy Johnson's Food Mart.
   (b) She went to the grocery store.
   (c) Allison was cheerful all the way to Johnson's Food Mart.
   (d) She cheerfully went to Johnson's Food Mart.

2. (a) Always concerned about his appearance, Alberto liked his new blue shirt.
   (b) Alberto liked his new shirt.
   (c) His shirt was new, and Alberto liked it.
   (d) His new shirt was blue; fortunately, Alberto liked it.

3. (a) The monkey hung from the bars of his cage.
   (b) Chattering, the monkey hung from the iron bars of his spacious cage.
   (c) The monkey hanging from the cage bars was chattering.
   (d) From the bars of his cage, the monkey hung.

4. (a) Everywhere sweet Mary went, she was followed by bleating lambs.
   (b) The lambs followed Mary everywhere.
   (c) Everywhere she went, lambs followed her.
   (d) Lambs were always following Mary everywhere.

5. (a) Tourists walked on a trail behind the waterfall.
   (b) There was a narrow, slippery trail behind the waterfall, and tourists walked on it.
   (c) Behind the Silver Falls Waterfall, brave tourists walked on a narrow, slippery trail.
   (d) A narrow, slippery trail behind the waterfall was walked on by tourists.

6. (a) Rising majestically from the plain, Mt. Shasta dominated the landscape.
   (b) The mountain dominated the landscape as it was rising from the plain.
   (c) Mt. Shasta was the main thing in the landscape.
   (d) In the landscape was the dominating mountain.

7. (a) He looked into the prism, and he saw all the colors of the rainbow.
   (b) He saw all the rainbow colors when he looked in the prism.
   (c) Looking into the prism, the wizard saw the rainbow colors.
   (d) Gazing into the prism, Walter the Wizard saw all the colors of the rainbow.

Assessment: Descriptive Language and Sentence Variety *(cont.)*

——— Sensory Words and Figurative Language ———

➤ In each group of sentences, fill in the circle by the one sentence that contains both the most effective sensory description (taste, feel, look, sound, smell) and figurative language (simile or metaphor).

1. (a) The tart lemon pie is like a wake-up call for my taste buds.
   (b) We gave the neighbors one of our lemon trees.
   (c) Very little of a lemon is used to make a lemon pie.
   (d) The lemons looked like Christmas decorations.

2. (a) Snakes can be very dangerous reptiles.
   (b) The Rocky Mountain rattlesnake's warning seemed as loud as thunder to me.
   (c) Rattlesnakes usually give a warning before they attack.
   (d) One kind of rattlesnake has diamonds on his back.

3. (a) My sunglasses make everything look rosy.
   (b) My sunglasses are not the latest style.
   (c) My thickly framed sunglasses are my gateway to a rose-colored world.
   (d) My old-fashioned sunglasses are heavy.

4. (a) A blank sheet of notepaper lay on the desk of the writer.
   (b) On the scarred oak desk lay a sheet of notepaper as white as snow.
   (c) A blank sheet of notepaper cannot be ignored by a writer.
   (d) Writers are known for not being able to ignore blank notepaper.

5. (a) Surfers at Cape Kiwanda Beach are very patient, waiting for the next wave.
   (b) Waiting for the next wave makes the Cape Kiwanda Beach surfers patient.
   (c) At Cape Kiwanda Beach, even an experienced surfer has to be very patient.
   (d) As patient as spiders in their webs, the Cape Kiwanda Beach surfers in their slick, black wetsuits waited for the next foamy wave to appear.

6. (a) Every time our doorbell sounds, our terrier begins a frightful howling.
   (b) Every time our doorbell rings, our terrier, Ringo, is like a howling wolf.
   (c) Our terrier becomes especially obnoxious when he hears the doorbell ring.
   (d) Ringo, our terrier, begins howling whenever he hears the doorbell ring.

7. (a) The banana slug is one of the ugliest, slimiest creatures in the world.
   (b) The yellow, slimy, six-inch long banana slug was clinging to the bark of the redwood tree like a leech.
   (c) The ugly, slimy banana slug can be found in the Hoh Rain Forest in the Olympic Peninsula in the state of Washington.
   (d) In the Hoh Rain Forest you can find many ugly, slimy banana slugs.

Paragraph Web

A paragraph consists of the following:

✧ a topic sentence that introduces the subject of the paragraph,

✧ body sentences or supporting details that expand or explain the topic sentence,

✧ a concluding sentence that expresses the main point of the paragraph.

➤ **Choose a topic you would like to write a short paragraph about. Use the form below to plan your paragraph.**

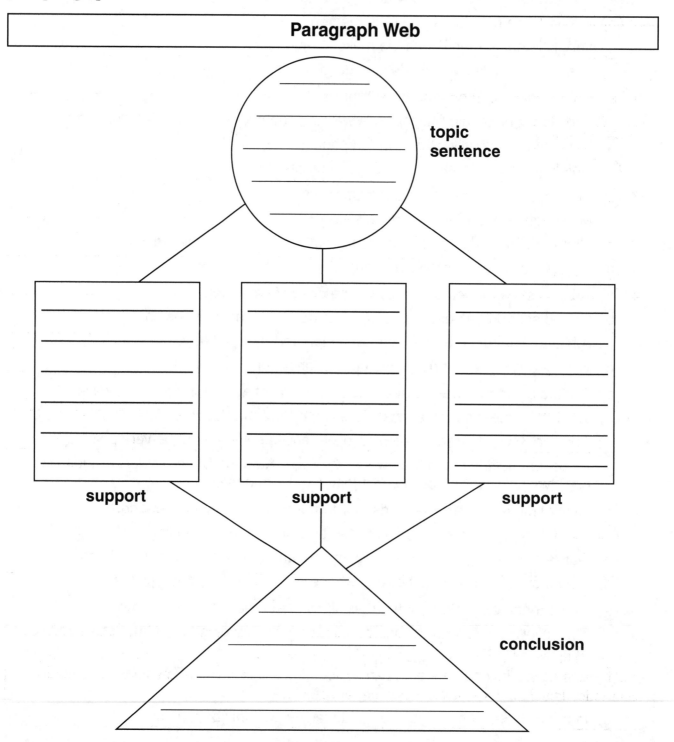

Paragraph Outline

➤ Use your paragraph web to write a paragraph outline. Add a title that is based on the topic sentence of your paragraph. For section II, write one general sentence about your three body sentences or supporting details. Then, A under II will be your first body sentence, B will be your second one, and C will be the third.

title _____

topic sentence

I. _____

_____

body sentences

II. _____

_____

A. _____

_____

B. _____

_____

C. _____

_____

concluding sentence

III. _____

_____

Use this outline as a guide when you write your paragraph on page 15. Remember that you may add ideas as you are writing; however, also remember that each addition must relate to or have a connection to the idea or sentence which comes before it.

Transition Words

Transition words are words that are used to connect two main ideas, showing that they are related in some way. When the following words are used as transitions between independent clauses, they are preceded by a semicolon and followed by a comma.

example: Alex was reluctant to go to the movie; **however***, I persuaded him to go.*

Function	Word or Phrase	
Add or emphasize an idea	• also • furthermore • in addition	• further • additionally
Indicate contrast or comparison	• however • though • instead of • yet	• nevertheless • similarly • on the other hand
Explain or illustrate	• for example • for instance • such as	• as though • then
Show a result or consequence	• accordingly • therefore • as a result • since	• consequently • because • so
Summarize	• in short • in conclusion • at last	• finally • last
Indicate order	• after • beforehand • later • afterward • earlier • next	• as soon as • finally • now • at the same time • immediately • first

Another helpful transition device is the use of synonyms. Also, using synonyms avoids repetition that a reader might find dull. For example, instead of describing a person as "bad" throughout a paragraph or essay, you might use "naughty," "evil," "wicked," or "villainous." When you are writing, it is always a good idea to have a dictionary and thesaurus available.

Transitions are also used in essays to guide the reader from one paragraph to the next. In the first sentence of a new paragraph, a writer might use a synonym for a word that was used in the last sentence of the paragraph just before. Another device is to repeat a key word.

example: (end of paragraph)   *That is one* **reason** *I think I should get the empty room instead of my brother.*

   (beginning of next paragraph)   *Another* **reason** *I have is the fact that I am older than he is.*

Paragraph

➤ Write your paragraph below, using the outline you wrote on page 13 as your guide. Use transitions to build bridges from sentence to sentence and lead your reader easily from one idea or detail to the next idea or detail. Try to include key transition words in your topic sentence and conclusion. Remember that synonyms can also be effective transitions.

*topic sentence example: I will never forget the very **first** time I saw my best **friend**.*

*concluding sentence example: **Finally**, we understand why we have become **comrades**.*

(Note the use of the word "comrades," a synonym for "friend.")

_____

_____

_____

_____

_____

_____

_____

_____

_____

_____

_____

Proofreading and Editing Checklist for Paragraphs

➢ Use this checklist to review and improve your paragraph on page 15.

- ❏ Prewriting, planning, organizing
- ❏ One main idea or topic
- ❏ List of supporting details in order
- ❏ Topic sentence developed
- ❏ Supporting sentences developed
- ❏ Concluding sentence developed
- ❏ Unrelated details removed
- ❏ Supporting details added
- ❏ Varied sentence structure
- ❏ Transitions used
- ❏ Word choice improved
- ❏ Similes and metaphors used
- ❏ Sensory words used
- ❏ Grammar checked
- ❏ Capitalization checked
- ❏ Punctuation checked
- ❏ Spelling checked

This checklist can be used to check every paragraph you write. It is also a good idea to look it over before you begin writing so that you can be thinking about what you need to do to make your paragraph as good as you possibly can. Also, you can use this checklist to evaluate paragraphs that others write.

Proofreading and Editing Checklist for Essays

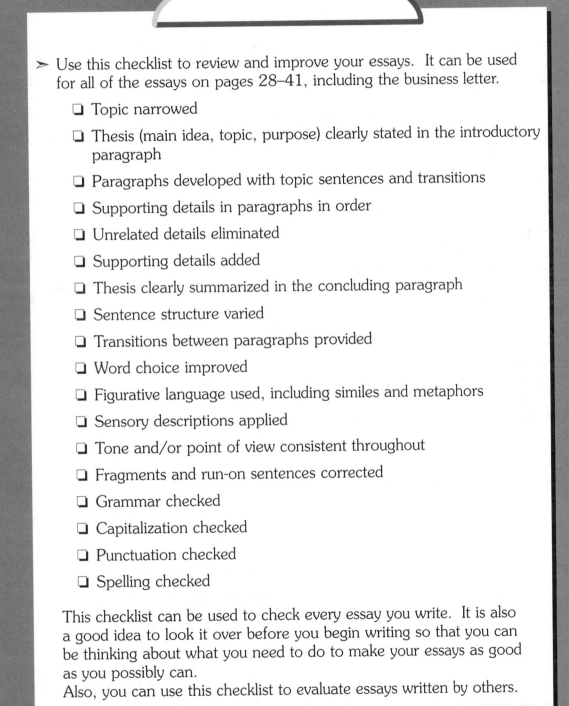

➤ Use this checklist to review and improve your essays. It can be used for all of the essays on pages 28–41, including the business letter.

❏ Topic narrowed

❏ Thesis (main idea, topic, purpose) clearly stated in the introductory paragraph

❏ Paragraphs developed with topic sentences and transitions

❏ Supporting details in paragraphs in order

❏ Unrelated details eliminated

❏ Supporting details added

❏ Thesis clearly summarized in the concluding paragraph

❏ Sentence structure varied

❏ Transitions between paragraphs provided

❏ Word choice improved

❏ Figurative language used, including similes and metaphors

❏ Sensory descriptions applied

❏ Tone and/or point of view consistent throughout

❏ Fragments and run-on sentences corrected

❏ Grammar checked

❏ Capitalization checked

❏ Punctuation checked

❏ Spelling checked

This checklist can be used to check every essay you write. It is also a good idea to look it over before you begin writing so that you can be thinking about what you need to do to make your essays as good as you possibly can.

Also, you can use this checklist to evaluate essays written by others.

Assessment: Paragraph Organization and Proofread and Edit

➤ Read the paragraph and answer the questions below. Fill in the circles beside the correct answers.

My Day at the Seashore

(1) Among my favorite places to visit is the beach. (2) I would not want to live there because I would not want to be cleaning sand out of my clothes and other belongings all the time. (3) It is a place where I can enjoy a variety of acitivities. (4) One of the things I like to do is to tease the waves. (5) By that I mean that I like to walk as close to the water as I can and still avoid getting wet. (6) However, I have been caught more than once by a wave that moves like a phantom. (7) A phantom wave is a wave that suddenly comes farther in to shore than the others. (8) Before I realize it. (9) Another thing I like to do is pick up unusual looking rocks. (10) At Mora Beach I found a rock that looks like an ice-cream cone. (11) The cone part is dark gray. (12) The ice-cream part is white. (13) I think I was really lucky to find such an odd rock. (14) Finally, I enjoy watching the birds. (15) The smaller water birds scurry around looking for good things to eat as they follow the waves that receede like retreating armies. (16) The larger birds such as the great blue herons stand still with their heads turned so that one eye is focused on the water as they search for prey.

(17) My day at the seashore seems incomplete if I am not chased by a phantom wave, do not discover a rock that seems diffrent from all the others, and no birds come to visit while I am there.

1. Which one of these words is used as a transition in sentence 4?
   ⓐ waves   ⓑ do   ⓒ tease   ⓓ One

2. Which one of the following sentences is a detail that can be omitted from the paragraph?
   ⓐ 9   ⓑ 3   ⓒ 2   ⓓ 14

3. Which group contains all three of the words misspelled in the paragraph?
   ⓐ phantom, diffrent, discover   ⓒ receede, scurry, acitivities
   ⓑ variety, heron, tease   ⓓ diffrent, receede, acitivities

4. Which one of the following sentences restates the main idea of the paragraph?
   ⓐ Sand and rocks are some of the writer's favorite items.
   ⓑ A good day is one spent with the waves, rocks, and birds at the ocean's shore.
   ⓒ Water birds are nearly always hungry when they are on the beach.
   ⓓ The writer's favorite ice-cream flavor is rocky road.

Assessment: Paragraph Organization and Proofread and Edit *(cont.)*

5. Which one of the following sentences could be added to the paragraph as a supporting detail?

    (a) They, too, are looking for any food the waves have left behind.

    (b) The mountains just are not as interesting to me as the beach is.

    (c) I once saw a hawk pounce on an unsuspecting rabbit.

    (d) Furthermore, the water is filled with all kinds of bacteria.

6. The kind of concluding sentence the author wrote is called which one of the following?

    (a) varied

    (b) transitional

    (c) summary

    (d) topic

7. Which group contains words that are used as transitions in the paragraph?

    (a) By that I mean, However, Finally

    (b) is, would want, like

    (c) I think, The smaller water birds

    (d) favorite, tease, avoid, looks

8. The word "odd" is a synonym for which one of these words in the paragraph?

    (a) phantom

    (b) unusual

    (c) rock

    (d) heron

9. A simile can be found in which one of these sentences?

    (a) 3

    (b) 5

    (c) 15

    (d) 17

10. Which one of these groups of words is a sentence fragment?

    (a) 2

    (b) 4

    (c) 6

    (d) 8

Sample Outline for a Three-Paragraph Essay

"My Day at the Seashore" on page 18 is an expository paragraph because it explains or gives reason why the author enjoys a day at the beach. It is possible to use the contents of a single paragraph to develop a three-paragraph or five-paragraph essay.

➤ The following is an outline for a three-paragraph essay based on "My Day at the Seashore." Compare the essay outline with the paragraph. Notice the added supporting details.

I. Among my favorite places to visit is the beach.
   A. There are several nearby beaches I can easily go to.
   B. The beach offers me several different things to do.
II. Some of the things I enjoy are teasing the waves, picking up unusual rocks, and watching the water birds.
   A. I like to walk as close to the edge of the water as possible without getting wet.
      1. I watch the waves closely and scamper away as they get close to me.
      2. Sometimes I get caught by a phantom wave.
         a. A phantom wave is one that surprises me.
         b. It is a wave that suddenly, without warning, comes in farther than the others.
   B. Picking up unusual rocks has become a hobby of mine.
      1. Recently, at Mora Beach I found a rock that looks like an ice-cream cone.
         a. The bottom part that is shaped like a cone is a rough, gray stone.
         b. The top part that represents the ice cream is a rounded white stone.
      2. One of my favorite rocks found at beaches is the colorful agate.
   C. Watching the shorebirds hunt for food is a pleasurable pastime.
      1. The smaller birds scurry after the waves to find the food that has washed ashore.
      2. The larger birds like the great blue heron are more dignified, standing patiently and waiting for their prey to swim by.
III. Being chased by phantom waves, picking up odd rocks, and watching the birds makes my day at the seashore just perfect.
   A. These are things I can do at nearly any beach I visit.
   B. The rocks, especially, help me remember each day by the seashore.

Outline Form Notes

Notice the form of an outline. The major divisions are indicated by Roman numerals. Capital letters are the next division, the third is Arabic numerals, and the fourth is lowercase letters. Each division contains more detailed information about the one before it.

Each division after the Roman numerals is indented. Numbers and letters of the same division are kept in a straight line down the page. A period is used after every number and letter.

Every outline must have at least two Roman numeral divisions. If there is an A division after a Roman numeral division, there must also be at least a B. If there is a 1 after an A or B or C, etc., there must also be a 2. If there is an a after a 1 or 2 or 3, there must also be a b.

Use the outlines on this page and the next page as guides when you compose your own outline in preparation for writing an essay.

Sample Outline for a Five-Paragraph Essay

The following is an outline for a five-paragraph essay based on "My Day at the Seashore," the paragraph on page 18.

➤ Compare this essay outline with the paragraph and with the outline for the three-paragraph essay to learn how the writer added supporting details to the three major divisions (II, III, and IV) of the topic. Note that the conclusion is a summary of those three major divisions and also restates the thesis and purpose (main idea or topic sentence) that is in the introduction (I).

I. Among my favorite places to visit is the beach.
   A. There are several nearby beaches I can reach easily.
   B. The beach has much to offer in the way of activities.

II. One of the things I like to do is to tease the waves as they come in.
   A. I like to walk as close to the edge of the water as possible.
   B. I watch the waves closely and scamper away as they get close to me.
   C. More than once I have been caught by a phantom wave.
      1. A phantom wave is one that surprises the beach walker.
      2. It is a wave that suddenly, without warning, comes farther in than the others.

III. Another thing I like to do is pick up unusual looking rocks.
   A. At Mora Beach in Washington I found a rock that looks like an ice-cream cone.
      1. The cone part is a rough, gray stone.
      2. The ice-cream part is a rounded white stone.
   B. At Agate Beach in Oregon I found colorful agates.
      1. These are called Oregon agates.
      2. I discovered shops in Oregon sell items made with the Oregon agates.

IV. Finally, I like to watch all the birds that gather at the seashore.
   A. Smaller water birds follow the waves out as they search for food.
      1. Their quick zig-zag movements amuse me.
      2. Sometimes they all fly up at the same time, making me wonder which one gave the signal.
   B. The larger great blue herons stand still with their heads turned so that one eye is focused on the water as they look for tender morsels for their meals.

V. All of these things make my day at the beach a very pleasurable one.
   A. Phantom waves chase me.
   B. I can pick up all the rocks my bag will hold.
   C. Watching the birds search for food is an engaging pastime.

Write an Outline for a Three-Paragraph Essay

➤ Use the contents of your outline on page 13, your paragraph on page 15, and additional supporting details to compose an outline for a three-paragraph essay.

Refer to the paragraph on page 18 and the outlines on pages 20 and 21. Remember to use correct outline form.

_____

_____

_____

_____

_____

_____

_____

_____

_____

_____

_____

_____

_____

_____

Write an Outline for a Five-Paragraph Essay

➤ Use the contents of your outline on page 13, your paragraph on page 15, your outline on page 22, and additional supporting details to compose an outline for a five-paragraph essay.

Refer to the paragraph on page 18 and the outlines on pages 20 and 21. Remember to use correct outline form.

Descriptions of Essays and Sample Topics

Expository Essay Description

An expository composition is one that explains or gives reasons. It may give the reader facts or explain the writer's ideas about a subject, or it may consist of directions or a series of steps. The purpose of exposition is to inform the reader; therefore, the purpose can be to explain "how to" do something or "why" something is done. For example, you might write an expository composition to explain how to prepare for a day at the beach, and then you might write one to tell why you like to go to the beach.

Sample Topics

Other topics you might use include the following:

◆ how to play a favorite sport
◆ why a certain sport is your favorite
◆ how to prepare for an earthquake
◆ why earthquakes occur
◆ how to plan for an invasion by Martians
◆ why Martians would like to visit Earth
◆ how to write a poem
◆ why you like to write poetry.

Narrative Essay Description

Narrative compositions are the details of an experience or of an event you witnessed. When telling about an experience or event, the writer usually starts at the beginning and tells what happened in the order in which it occurred—chronological (or time) order. Many times the experience or event calls for the writer to relate not only what others did but also what they said. That means that both direct quotations and indirect speech are often included in narratives. Narratives can be about events that really happened (nonfiction), or they can be about events that you make up (fiction). However, good advice for writers—both beginning and experienced ones—is to write about what they know best or firsthand. That means writing about events you have actually participated in or observed.

Sample Topics

These are topics others have used for a narrative composition:

◆ the first time you ever babysat or rode a horse or cooked dinner for your family
◆ memories of an embarrassing or frightening or exciting event
◆ memories of your first day of school or last birthday party or the day a baby brother or sister joined your family.

Descriptions of Essays and Sample Topics (cont.)

Autobiographical Essay Description

Though both expository and narrative topics may be autobiographical, they are not required to be. To write an autobiographical essay, you must tell about something that actually occurred in your own life. For a short composition, choose an event that takes place in a relatively short period of time. Remember that you will want to include specific details and descriptions.

Sample Topics

All of the sample topics for narratives could also be used for autobiographical compositions. Other ideas follow:

- ✧ visits with relatives
- ✧ moving with your family from one place to another community or state or country
- ✧ sharing a room with a brother or sister
- ✧ riding on a bus or train or airplane for the first time
- ✧ having a part in a play or skit
- ✧ hiking and camping in the woods.

Biographical Essay Description

To write a biographical essay, you must tell about something that actually occurred in someone else's life. That person should be someone you know well enough so that you do not have to do any more research than just a few questions to be sure that you have some of your facts correct. Otherwise, if you were to choose someone you do not know well, the result would be a research paper because you would have to go to a variety of sources to learn about the subject of your composition. On the other hand, you could base a biographical essay on an interview where you prepare a series of questions for a person you are acquainted with but do not know well. The answers to the questions would then become part of the content of your essay.

Sample Topics

You could choose these people to write about:

- ✧ any family member
- ✧ a neighbor
- ✧ a close friend
- ✧ a teacher
- ✧ anyone you come in contact with regularly.

Usually, you would choose someone you can reach easily in case you want to ask that person some questions. Of course, you could write about the life of your dog or your pet parrot, too. In that case, you already have all the answers. If you should decide to base your composition on an interview of someone you do not know well, your questions should be carefully thought out and organized and prepared with a specific, limited purpose. That is, you do not want to write about a 60-year-old person's entire life—or even a 20-year-old or an eight-year-old person's entire life.

Descriptions of Essays and Sample Topics *(cont.)*

Persuasive Essay Description

A persuasive essay is one you write to try to get your readers to agree with your point of view about a subject. You decide that you are for or against something or that you think one way is better than another. Then, you use the best reasons you can think of to persuade your readers to have the same opinion. For this essay, you will want to think about your reasons and about the order to put them in when you outline your essay. Usually, you will want to save your strongest and best reason or argument for the last, since it is the last thing you write that your readers are most likely to remember the best.

Sample Topics

Again, write about what you know. Think of the subjects that you talk about when you try to get your parents to see things your way. For example, you might discuss these topics with them:

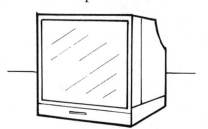

* ✧ required household chores
* ✧ amount of your allowance or pay for chores
* ✧ how late you can stay up
* ✧ music you are permitted to listen to
* ✧ television shows you are permitted to watch.

Also, you might want to persuade your teacher to think the way you do about some things: amount of homework or grading scale, for example. Perhaps you want to persuade your friends to go to a certain movie or play a certain game. All those would be good topics for persuasive essays.

Book Report Essay

When writing an essay about a book that you have read, be sure to take these steps:

* Describe the book. Give the title and the author's name and tell what kind of book it is: a novel, a biography, etc. Tell who you think the book was written for. Was it written for readers who are interested in stories about horses? Was it written for readers who like to read about the lives of Native-American leaders such as Geronimo?

* Tell about the author. Give not only the author's name but also tell something about the author. That could be the titles of other books the author has written or any writing awards the author has received. Many times there is a place in the front or back of a book where biographical information is given about an author.

* Describe the setting, main characters, and the conflict (if there is one). Let your reader know where the activity in the book is taking place and who the main characters are. If the book has a plot, do not give a detailed description—but you can let your reader know if there are any conflicts. For example, has a young boy been given a wild horse to try to tame? Has a Native-American leader been betrayed by men and leaders that he trusted?

* Compare the book to others you have read. If you have read other books by the same author, tell how they are similar to and/or different from the one you are writing about. Also, if you have read a book about the same subject by a different author, you can compare that book with the one you are writing about.

Descriptions of Essays and Sample Topics (cont.)

Book Report Essay (cont.)

• Give your opinion of the book. Tell whether you think the author's characters seemed realistic or whether the information was interesting. Let your reader know whether you would like to read other books by the same author.

You can use the above information as a guide when you compose your outline for your book report essay. (For example, your description of the book could be used for I, information about the author could be under II, etc.)

Sample Topics

You could write about a book that you have read for a class assignment or about any book that you have chosen to read that is appropriate for you and others your age. Some books that would be considered by many parents and teachers to be appropriate for most sixth graders are the following:

✦ *The Call of the Wild* by Jack London

✦ *Sing Down the Moon* by Scott O'Dell

✦ *Hatchet* by Gary Paulsen

✦ *The Secret Garden* by Frances Hodgson Burnett

✦ *By the Great Horn Spoon* by Sid Fleischman

✦ *Dear Mr. Henshaw* by Beverly Cleary

✦ *Misty of Chincoteague* by Marguerite Henry

✦ *The Black Stallion* by Walter Farley

Business Letter

When composing a business letter, there are two main things to remember: The first one is that you should immediately state your purpose for writing. The second one is that you should tell the reader exactly what it is that you are requesting from the business or businessperson you are writing to. Your use of language should be exact, and you should be polite. Remember to give all the specific details of the matter you are writing about. For example, if you are writing to order an item, be sure to give all the information that you have available about that item—size, color, etc. Usually, a business letter is short and to the point and not more than one page long. Do not think that you have to fill an entire page when you are writing a business letter.

If you are responding to a business letter, be sure to first give exactly any information that is asked for. After that, you may give further information if you think it is needed and if you are sure that it is appropriate. Be sure to use the name and title of the person who signed the letter when you write the inside address and the address on the envelope. Also, use the person's name in the greeting of your letter.

Sample Topics

Business letters are written for a variety of purposes. Below is a list of possibilities:

✦ to a state's board of tourism to request vacation information

✦ to the National Park Service to request information about a specific national park

✦ to your representative or senator to request a meeting with him/her when you are in Washington, D.C.

✦ to a company to complain about the service you received when you made a purchase in that company's store

✦ to a company to compliment an employee who gave you good service

✦ to respond to an inquiry about baseball cards/Barbie dolls you have for sale

✦ to your local fire department, police department, or newspaper to inquire whether that organization gives tours for school groups.

Write an Expository Essay

✧ Choose a topic for an expository essay. Refer to the description and sample topics on page 24.
✧ Develop a topic sentence.
✧ Make a list of ideas and supporting details.
✧ Compose a concluding sentence.

topic sentence

_____

_____

list of ideas and supporting details

_____

_____

_____

_____

_____

_____

_____

_____

_____

_____

concluding sentence

_____

_____

Write an Expository Essay *(cont.)*

➤ Put the contents of your list into outline form. Refer to the sample outlines on pages 20 and 21. You may prepare an outline for a three- or four- or five-paragraph essay.

outline

_____

_____

_____

_____

_____

_____

_____

_____

_____

_____

_____

_____

_____

✧ Decide on a title for your essay.

✧ Using your outline as your guide, write a first or rough draft of your essay.

✧ Use the checklist on page 17 as you revise, edit, and proofread your essay.

✧ Write and proofread the final copy of your essay.

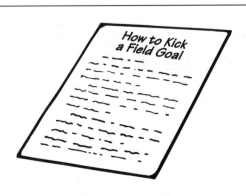

Write a Narrative Essay

- ❖ Choose a topic for a narrative essay. Refer to the description and sample topics on page 24.
- ❖ Develop a topic sentence.
- ❖ Make a list of ideas and supporting details.
- ❖ Compose a concluding sentence.

topic sentence

_____

_____

list of ideas and supporting details

_____

_____

_____

_____

_____

_____

_____

_____

_____

_____

_____

concluding sentence

_____

_____

Write a Narrative Essay *(cont.)*

➤ Put the contents of your list into outline form. Refer to the sample outlines on pages 20 and 21. You may prepare an outline for a three- or four- or five-paragraph essay.

outline

_____

_____

_____

_____

_____

_____

_____

_____

_____

_____

_____

_____

✧ Decide on a title for your essay.

✧ Using your outline as your guide, write a first or rough draft of your essay.

✧ Use the checklist on page 17 as you revise, edit, and proofread your essay.

✧ Write and proofread the final copy of your essay.

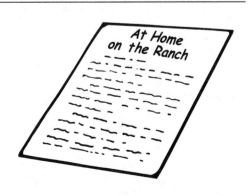

Write an Autobiographical Essay

✧ Choose a topic for an autobiographical essay. Refer to the description and sample topics on pages 24 and 25.

✧ Develop a topic sentence.

✧ Make a list of ideas and supporting details.

✧ Compose a concluding sentence.

topic sentence

_____

_____

list of ideas and supporting details

_____

_____

_____

_____

_____

_____

_____

_____

_____

_____

concluding sentence

_____

_____

Write an Autobiographical Essay (cont.)

➤ Put the contents of your list into outline form. Refer to the sample outlines on pages 20 and 21. You may prepare an outline for a three- or four- or five-paragraph essay.

outline

_____

_____

_____

_____

_____

_____

_____

_____

_____

_____

_____

_____

✧ Decide on a title for your essay.

✧ Using your outline as your guide, write a first or rough draft of your essay.

✧ Use the checklist on page 17 as you revise, edit, and proofread your essay.

✧ Write and proofread the final copy of your essay.

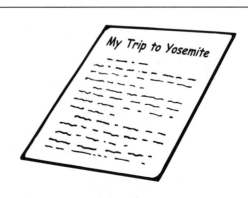

Write a Biographical Essay

✧ Choose a topic for a biographical essay. Refer to the description and sample topics on page 25.
✧ Develop a topic sentence.
✧ Make a list of ideas and supporting details.
✧ Compose a concluding sentence.

| topic sentence |

_____

_____

| list of ideas and supporting details |

_____

_____

_____

_____

_____

_____

_____

_____

_____

_____

| concluding sentence |

_____

_____

Write a Biographical Essay *(cont.)*

➤ Put the contents of your list into outline form. Refer to the sample outlines on pages 20 and 21. You may prepare an outline for a three- or four- or five-paragraph essay.

| outline |

_____

_____

_____

_____

_____

_____

_____

_____

_____

_____

_____

_____

_____

✧ Decide on a title for your essay.

✧ Using your outline as your guide, write a first or rough draft of your essay.

✧ Use the checklist on page 17 as you revise, edit, and proofread your essay.

✧ Write and proofread the final copy of your essay.

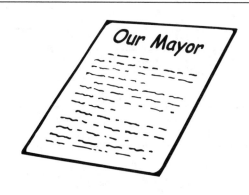

Write a Persuasive Essay

✧ Choose a topic for a persuasive essay. Refer to the description and sample topics on page 26.
✧ Develop a topic sentence.
✧ Make a list of ideas and supporting details.
✧ Compose a concluding sentence.

| topic sentence |

_____

_____

| list of ideas and supporting details |

_____

_____

_____

_____

_____

_____

_____

_____

_____

_____

_____

| concluding sentence |

_____

_____

Write a Persuasive Essay *(cont.)*

➤ Put the contents of your list into outline form. Refer to the sample outlines on pages 20 and 21. You may prepare an outline for a three- or four- or five-paragraph essay

outline

_____

_____

_____

_____

_____

_____

_____

_____

_____

_____

_____

_____

_____

❖ Decide on a title for your essay.

❖ Using your outline as your guide, write a first or rough draft of your essay.

❖ Use the checklist on page 17 as you revise, edit, and proofread your essay.

❖ Write and proofread the final copy of your essay.

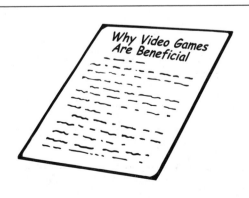

Write a Book Report Essay

- ✧ Choose a topic for a book report essay. Refer to the description and sample topics on pages 26 and 27.
- ✧ Develop a topic sentence.
- ✧ Make a list of ideas and supporting details.
- ✧ Compose a concluding sentence.

| topic sentence |

_____

_____

| list of ideas and supporting details |

_____

_____

_____

_____

_____

_____

_____

_____

_____

_____

_____

| concluding sentence |

_____

_____

Write a Book Report Essay *(cont.)*

➤ Put the contents of your list into outline form. Refer to the sample outlines on pages 20 and 21. You may prepare an outline for a three- or four- or five-paragraph essay.

outline

_____

_____

_____

_____

_____

_____

_____

_____

_____

_____

_____

_____

_____

✧ Decide on a title for your essay. Do not use the title of the book alone for your essay title, but it is okay to use the book title in your essay title.

   Example: Horse Lovers Will Enjoy *Black Stallion*

✧ Using your outline as your guide, write a first or rough draft of your essay.

✧ Use the checklist on page 17 as you revise, edit, and proofread your essay.

✧ Write and proofread the final copy of your essay.

Write a Business Letter

✧ Choose a purpose for a business letter. Refer to the description and sample purposes on page 27.

✧ **Heading:** Write your street address on the first line and your city, state, and zip code on the second line. On the third line, write the date of the letter. (**Note:** If you are using a word processor, you can create a heading that includes your full name on the first line, making four lines for the heading.)

✧ **Inside Address:** Write the name of the company or the name of the businessperson on the first line. If you are using the businessperson's name, you separate it from the name of the company with a comma. Use the second line for the company's street address and the third line for the city, state, and zip code.

✧ **Greeting:** If you do not use a person's name in the inside address, use a general greeting such as "Dear Sir:" or "Dear Madam:."

✧ **Body:** Refer to the description on page 27. The body of your business letter, unlike an essay, may have only one or two paragraphs. Each paragraph may consist of only one to three sentences. (**Note:** If you are making a request, be sure to use the words "please" and "thank you" in your letter.)

✧ **Closing:** You may use "Sincerely," "Sincerely yours," or "Very truly yours" for the closing in a business letter.

✧ **Signature:** Sign your full name directly below the closing.

➤ On the lines below, write the body of your business letter.

_____

_____

_____

_____

_____

_____

_____

_____

_____

_____

Write a Business Letter *(cont.)*

➤ Write a rough draft of your business letter below.

_____

_____

_____

_____

_____

_____

_____

_____

_____

_____

_____

_____

_____

_____

_____

_____

_____

_____

❖ Use the checklist on page 17 as you revise, edit, and proofread your business letter.

❖ Write and proofread the final copy of your business letter.

Evaluation Checklist for Paragraphs and Essays

➤ To evaluate your own paragraphs and essays as well as those written by others, you can use the following checklist as a guide.

❏ 1. The title reveals or suggests the topic of the composition.

❏ 2. There is one main idea or topic stated in the introduction.

❏ 3. All of the content relates directly to the main idea.

❏ 4. The main idea is summarized or restated in the conclusion.

❏ 5. Sentence structure is varied.

❏ 6. Transitions are used throughout the composition.

❏ 7. Word choice is appropriate.

❏ 8. Figurative language makes comparisons interesting.

❏ 9. Sensory words make descriptions more vivid.

❏ 10. The tone is consistent throughout.

❏ 11. Point of view is consistent throughout.

❏ 12. There are no sentence fragments.

❏ 13. There are no run-on sentences.

❏ 14. Grammar is used correctly.

❏ 15. Capitalization is correct.

❏ 16. Punctuation is correct.

❏ 17. All words are spelled correctly.

❏ 18. The composition has a clear introduction, body, and conclusion.

❏ 19. Supporting details have been added and are organized.

❏ 20. No unrelated details are included.

Evaluation of an Essay

Use the evaluation checklist on page 42 to evaluate one of the essays you wrote for Section 6 (pages 24–41): expository, narrative, autographical, biographical, persuasive, and book report. (Do not use the business letter.)

- Underline or mark in some other way examples of transitions, similes and metaphors, and sensory words. Also mark the main idea in both the introduction and the conclusion.

- Use a different marking method for any sentence structure you think you could improve, any place where you think a transition is needed, and any word choice that could be upgraded. Also, make note of any sentence fragments or run-on sentences and any grammar, capitalization, punctuation, or spelling errors. If there are any unrelated details that should be omitted, mark those also.

- The information you marked and noted is to be part of the content for an evaluation paragraph about your essay. Compare the way your main idea is stated in your introduction with the way you restated it in your conclusion. Tell your reader some of the transitions, similes and metaphors, and sensory words you used. Point out any content that you think is especially interesting and would appeal to most readers of your essay.

- Next, give suggestions for improving your essay. Do fragments and run-on sentences need to be corrected? Does your essay lack sensory descriptions? Does your conclusion do a poor job of restating or summarizing your main idea? Point out any weaknesses you find and explain what you can do to improve the quality of your essay.

- Finally, for your conclusion, tell your reader which one of the following categories you think is the correct one for your essay:

_____ **outstanding**   _____ **good**   _____ **satisfactory**   _____ **revise and rewrite**

Outline your evaluation paragraph below and then write the final copy on a separate sheet of paper.

_____

_____

_____

_____

_____

_____

_____

_____

Unit Assessment

➤ **In each group of sentences, fill in the circle beside the sentence with the correct grammar, punctuation, capitalization, and spelling.**

1. (a) My younger brother is better in Science than I am?

    (b) He is also better at such sportes as Baseball and Basketball.

    (c) However, I can still run faster than he can.

    (d) Someday soon, He will probably be able to beet me in a race!

2. (a) If we lived in the country, I could have a dog and a horse.

    (b) If I had a dog, I wood name him spot and name my horse silver.

    (c) The kinds of dog I wood like to have is a German shepperd.

    (d) My Mother says that I wont get either one very soon.

3. (a) Memorial day is a day to rember all those who fought for freedom.

    (b) Memorial Day is a Day to rember all those who fought for freedom.

    (c) Memorial Day is a day to remember all those who fought for freedom.

    (d) Memorial Day is a day to rember all those whom fought for freedom.

4. (a) Get over here right now, my Father called to my Brother.

    (b) "Get over here right now!" my father called to my brother.

    (c) "Get over here rite now!" My Father called to my brother.

    (d) Get over here rite now! my father called to my brother.

5. (a) I wanted to go to Hiouchi's birthday party but I had the flue.

    (b) I wanted to go to Hiouchi's birthday party, but I had the flue.

    (c) I wanted to go to Hiouchis birthday party, but I had the flu.

    (d) I wanted to go to Hiouchi's birthday party, but I had the flu.

➤ **In each pair of sentences, fill in the circle beside the sentence which has a simile or metaphor in it.**

6. (a) Doris does not like to ride on the rollercoaster.

    (b) She says riding it is like trying to stay on a bucking horse.

7. (a) I will think that my friend Patsy is as foolish as Jane if she does not take advantage of the offer.

    (b) I will think that my friend Patsy is just like Jane, who is a fish in a ring of alligators.

8. (a) Every morning the squawking jaybird is my alarm clock.

    (b) Every morning the squawking jaybird wakes me up.

Unit Assessment *(cont.)*

9. (a) When my sister yells at me she brays like a donkey.

    (b) When my sister yells at me she makes me think of a donkey.

10. (a) My older brother was too cowardly to confess he broke the dish.

    (b) My older brother is a skunk for being too cowardly to confess he broke the dish.

➢ **In each pair of sentences, fill in the circle beside the sentence which would be the better topic sentence for a persuasive composition.**

11. (a) I do not think that my younger brother should get his own room before I do.

    (b) The other day I saw the furniture that I would like for my room.

12. (a) Last year our family went to both Disneyland and Magic Mountain.

    (b) Disneyland is a better place for a family to go than Magic Mountain.

13. (a) I have never been anywhere on either a train or an airplane.

    (b) Travel by train is more stimulating than travel by airplane.

14. (a) I would rather have my birthday party at a park than at home.

    (b) I went to a birthday party at Tri-Cities Park last week.

15. (a) I have been getting an allowance from my parents since I was five years old.

    (b) Because I am such a hard worker and good student, my allowance should be raised.

➢ **Fill in the circle beside the correct outline form.**

16. a I.
    ○   A.
          B.
               1.
          C.

    b I.
    ○   A.
          B.
      II.
          A.
          B.
          C.
      III.
          A.
          B.

(c) I.
        A.
        B.
    II.
        A.
          1.
          2.
          3.
    III.

(d) I.
        A.
        B.
          1.
    II.
        A.
        B.

Unit Assessment *(cont.)*

➤ **Read the paragraph and answer the questions that follow it. Fill in the circles beside the correct answers.**

A Sunday Picnic in the Redwoods

(1) Because it was such a welcoming spring morning with the sun shining brightly on the golden California poppies, we decided to go on a Sunday picnic. (2) We packed a lunch of bananas and crunchy Fuji apples, sharp cheddar cheese and wheat crackers, and sweet peanut butter cookies. (3) Then, we began our one-mile hike to Jedediah Smith State Park. (4) As we turned toward the park picnic area, we noticed the pink and white flowers at the feet of the soaring redwood trees. (5) Those blooming trilliums were a colorful carpet on the floor of the forest. (6) When we reached the bank of the Smith River, we emerged into the sunshine again. (7) Before us was a small, sandy beach. (8) As we drew closer, we saw a father playing with his three young children at the edge of the river. (9) The water was clear and as green as sparkling emeralds. (10) However, even though the sunshine was warm, the water was as cold as ice. (11) The children would stick their toes into the water and then run, laughing, back to the warmth of the sand. (12) By the time we finished our lunch at one of the picnic tables beside the river, the children and father were packing up their beach toys and towels and getting into their car to leave. (13) All of us had enjoyed the sunny spring day. (14) We really liked the cheese.

---

17. Which kind of paragraph is "A Sunday Picnic in the Redwoods"?

    ⓐ narrative

    ⓑ persuasive

    ⓒ biographical

    ⓓ expository

18. Which sentence contains a simile?

    ⓐ 1   ⓑ 3   ⓒ 8   ⓓ 9

Answer Key

Page 4

1. You're (or You are) the first one in your family to have a bicycle of your very own.

2. Jane Smith, Kim Choi, and Sitara Jaworski went to Lakewood Mall to buy new clothes.

3. (correct)

4. They were the very last ones to leave the room on Valentine's Day.

5. Are you the heir to your wealthy uncle's estate?

6. We don't (or do not) want to go to the party later.

7. Jerry had his paper with him, but he didn't (or did not) have his pencil.

8. Ari isn't ever going shopping with those girls again.

9. There are hardly any differences among those three girls.

10. On Independence Day we went (or had gone) to the Colorado River with our friends.

11. "Hurry, hurry!" Mother yelled. "I need help with these (or those) groceries."

12. (correct)

Page 5

1. c
2. c
3. d
4. b
5. d
6. c
7. a
8. d

Pages 6–9

Answers will vary.

Page 10

1. a
2. a
3. b
4. a
5. c

6. a
7. d

Page 11

1. a
2. b
3. c
4. b
5. d
6. b
7. b

Pages 18 and 19

1. d
2. c
3. d
4. b
5. a
6. c
7. a
8. b
9. c
10. d

Pages 44–47

1. c	13. b
2. a	14. a
3. c	15. b
4. b	16. b
5. d	17. a
6. b	18. d
7. b	19. b
8. a	20. b
9. a	21. d
10. b	22. c
11. a	23. b
12. b	24. b

Unit Assessment *(cont.)*

19. Which sentence contains a metaphor?
    - (a) 2
    - (b) 5
    - (c) 6
    - (d) 9

20. Which of the following words in sentence 10 is used as a transition?
    - (a) even
    - (b) However
    - (c) was
    - (d) cold

21. Which of the following sentences should be omitted from the paragraph?
    - (a) 2
    - (b) 3
    - (c) 11
    - (d) 14

22. Which of the following words is used as a sensory word in sentence 1?
    - (a) welcoming
    - (b) sun
    - (c) golden
    - (d) picnic

23. Which of the following sentences begins with a transition?
    - (a) 2
    - (b) 3
    - (c) 9
    - (d) 11

24. Which of the following could also be used as the title of the paragraph?
    - (a) Eating Cheese at the Smith River
    - (b) Spring Sunday by the Smith River
    - (c) Sandy Beach and Cold Water
    - (d) Trilliums Bloom in the Forest